Other books by the author:

The Chocoverse Trilogy:
Free Chocolate
Pure Chocolate
Fake Chocolate

Cookbook:
There are Herbs in My Chocolate

Story Like a Journalist:
A Workbook for Novelists

Volume 1:

Story Bible Overview

Amber Royer

GOLDEN TIP
PRESS

Golden Tip Press

A Golden Tip Press Instructional Series original 2020

Copyright ©2020 by Amber Royer

All rights reserved. No part of this publication may be reproduced, stored in a retrieval system, or transmitted in any for or by any means, electronic, mechanical, photocopying, recording, or otherwise, without the prior written permission of the publisher.

Cover art and editorial design: Amber Royer

Printing: IngramSpark

Published by Golden Tip Press
1520 Ridhardson Dr
#1311
Richardson, TX 75080

ISBN 978-0-9914083-8-2

Introduction 7

Chapter One: Your Story Bible -- The Entry Point to Your Story World 8

   Putting Everything in Order 8

      Strategies for Building Your Story Bible 8

         Do You Need A Full Story Bible? Checklist (A-1) 10

      Where to Keep Your Notes 10

         Story Bible Overarching Worksheet (O-1) 12

   Compiling a Story Bible 12

         Named Characters List (A-2) 13

         Invented Objects and Places List (A-3) 13

      Determining Narration 13

         Narration Worksheet (A-4) 16

      Determining Point of View 17

         POV Worksheet (A-5) 20

      Setting the Rules 20

         Setting Rules for Your World Worksheet (A-6) 24

         Determining Ease Worksheet (A-7) 24

      Making Promises 25

         Promises to the Reader Worksheet (A-8) 27

   Lessons from the Journalism Classroom 28

      Be Clear and Unbiased 28

         Who Has Agency Worksheet (A-9) 29

      Do Your Research 29

         Research Questions Worksheet (A-10) 31

      Verify Your Sources 31

         Bibliography Worksheet (A-11) 32

      Mine the Real World for Story Ideas 33

         Real World Story Ideas List (A-12) 34

         Idea Generation Worksheet (A-13) 34

Define Your Angle 35
    Angle Worksheet (A-14) 36
    Genre Conversation Worksheet (A-15) 37
    Idea Mashups Worksheet (A-16) 37
Don't Bury the Lede 37
    Novelist's Lede Worksheet (A-17) 38
Write Straightforward Sentences and Scenes 38
    Imagery Worksheet (A-18) 41
    Body Language Observation Worksheet (A-19) 41
    Blocking Worksheet (A-20) 42
    Storyboarding Worksheet (A-21) 42
Use Quotes 42
    Language Overview Worksheet (A-22) 45
    Lexicon Worksheet (A-23) 45
    Jargon Worksheet (A-24) 46
    Word Choice Chart (A-25) 46

Introduction

Story Like a Journalist Vol 1 – Story Bible Overview

Get ready to get organized and plan your novel. Having a plan in place for how you will approach your project can save you time and minimize the need for re-writes. But where to start, when maybe you've just got a couple of characters standing around, and a vague idea of where you want the story to end?

You need to generate ideas — and then set limits on those ideas. Otherwise, once you unlock your imagination, you can get overwhelmed by the sheer possibilities presented.

Making decisions early in the process — on the type of story you are telling, on how many of your fictional people are telling the story, on whether they are telling it in the now or distant past — can actually work to reduce anxiety as you write. Start determining boundaries and setting rules, and suddenly you have a list if right answers to look at when you're not sure how to handle a particular scene. Same goes for specifics about the story. Character names, places they live — narrowing things down takes the pressure off.

But if you get started and something isn't working, you can always go back and re-work those rules. That first-person narrator you wanted to tell the whole story can't show up at an important event, because nobody told her it is happening? Go back and change to plan, so that you will write in third. Realize that you can't actually pronounce Yvkkstlmd's name if you ever have to read this out loud? Go back and give him some vowels, or change his name to Yav. You're setting limits to make your writing life easier, after all.

Approach planning your novel the way a journalist plans out writing a news piece. They figure out what they will need to research for the piece, and decide how they will structure that research into a narrative. They decide on a format for the story's lede (opening designed to draw the reader in) and structure the story to follow up on the questions presented in that lede. They document everything, so that they can verify the accuracy of everything they present.

Think like a journalist as you build your novel's Story Bible, a document that organizes everything else about what you will write. Are you ready to get started?

Your Story Bible -- The Entry Point to Your Story World

Putting Everything in Order

Approach planning your novel the way a journalist plans out writing a news piece. They figure out what they will need to research for the piece, and decide how they will structure that research into a narrative. They decide on a format for the story's lede (opening designed to draw the reader in) and structure the story to follow up on the questions presented in that lede. They document everything, so that they can verify the accuracy of everything they present.

Think like a journalist as you build your novel's Story Bible, a document that organizes everything else about what you will write. Are you ready to get started?

A Journalist Asks: What should I write about? What will readers/viewers be most interested in? What makes this story newsworthy? How should I approach writing it? What elements of the larger topic belong in this story?

A Novelist Asks: What should I write about? What will my readers find interesting about my novel's idea? What will this novel add to my genre, or say in a new way? How will I approach narration? What am I promising my readers that this story will follow up on?

A Story Bible is a detailed plan for your story. It will help you:

-- Stay on track for building and pacing your novel.

-- Create a reference source full of information about how your story world works, to look at to see connections and spark ideas.

-- Stay consistent as you introduce character traits, character appearance and setting details.

-- Set limits for what plot events CAN happen, so that you can figure out what SHOULD happen.

-- Write a cleanly-plotted first draft that reflects an understanding of your characters from the very beginning.

The first step to designing a Story Bible is to decide on a basic strategy.

Strategies for Building Your Story Bible

Some stories are straightforward, with only a handful of characters and only a few settings. If this is the case, you may be able to do an abbreviated form of a

Story Bible. But there are other considerations, such as whether your characters are part of a group with specialized skills and jargon. Think about how complex your story really might be, if you consider all its aspects.

Structure that Won't Hamper Creativity

Remember: just because you wrote it in the novel plan document, doesn't mean it's canon – yet. For a novelist, the Story Bible is in complete flux until the first volume is published. If you come up with better ideas as you write, don't be afraid to explore them. The planning stage is meant to help you feel like you have a real world to refer to, to give you right answers when you look something up – not to stifle your creativity. Honestly, you're not likely to follow your initial novel plan completely. The document needs to be updated as details, character relationships, and plot elements change. Try to do this as you write, especially if you start to diverge from your original outline. Otherwise you may have trouble remembering what was part of the original idea, and what is part of the revision.

Approach for Planners

You can work through the Story Bible first – or you can discovery write a chapter or two worth of your initial ideas, come back to the workbook and start filling in the worksheets as they apply to what you want to write next. Either way, keep your Story Bible handy as you work. As you write the draft, add details and statistics to your Story Bible document.

Consistency and accuracy are the key benefits you get from drafting alongside a complete Story Bible. It can also save you time in the long run, because you won't have to look up small details in the manuscript, such as whether your antagonist's eyes were green or blue six chapters ago.

Approach for Discovery Writers

It is possible to build a Story Bible after you've written your draft. And while it may seem counterintuitive, it can still be beneficial to do the exercises in this workbook after the fact. If you discovery-wrote the manuscript, the sheer act of compiling a Story Bible can help you consider:

> -- What **possible contradictions** do you need to address?
> *Example:* Do your aliens eat insects in chapter 12 or are they vegetarians like you said in chapter 4?

-- Do you have **too many characters?**
Example: Maybe the protagonist doesn't need six guy friends, when three serve as sounding boards.

-- What **backstory** do you need to delve deeper into?
Example: Why exactly did your protagonist cut her mother out of her life? She feels erratic if you don't tell us.

-- Where might there be **plot holes** and **oversights**?

Example: How did your protagonist know that the gun was in the sewer grate? Better go back and foreshadow.

Do You Need A Full Story Bible? Checklist (A-1)
Consider the questions on the checklist to determine if you need a full Story Bible.

Concerns – Put a checkmark by anything you have been trying to improve, or anything that you aren't sure how to complete.

Aspects – Put a checkmark by features of the novel project you have in mind that might make it more complex.

If you answer yes to a couple of these questions, work through the Story Bible Overarching Worksheet above, which organizes information from the other worksheets in the book to allow you to systematically build a detailed novel plan.

If you answer no to all of the questions, scan through the worksheets under each section and fill out the ones that will help you with your current project.

Where to Keep Your Notes

There's no right or wrong way to organize – as long as you do organize. Even if you are a discovery writer, there's a lot to a novel, and you are looking at more consistency re-writes if you try to keep it all in your head than if you lay it out logically.

Paper Notebooks – Keep the notebook on you/your bedside table to record information as you think of it. On one level, novel writing is like building and solving an enormous puzzle at the same time. Pieces of it often come together hours after a productive writing session (along with oversights and conflicts you haven't yet taken into consideration). Some people prefer paper notebooks for all their projects. I do paper when I need to see info graphically and draw in connections. I also make paper maps.

Notes Applications – You can create a virtual notebook, with a separate note for each topic your Story Bible covers, along with a "to fix" note. There are a number of notes programs, but I like Evernote because it has a free version and I can access the notes on my computer to directly paste things I've written into my manuscript file. I prefer to take most of my notes on my phone using this app then delete them after I have updated the manuscript or moved the information into my project wiki.

In-manuscript notes – If I've left a gap where I need to add a scene or other information, or I need to do research to verify the history or physics involved, I make a note directly in the manuscript. I highlight these notes, and at the end of the writing session, I address what I can, and then I add any relevant info to my Evernote file. Notes can be made directly in the body of the manuscript, or if you are using Word or a similar word processing software there is a notes feature that allows you to make notes in the margins. These notes can even be sent as part of the file, so that another user can edit them.

Scrivener – The notecard view in this writing software is great for organizing information. The color-coding feature here adds to the usability. You can move the notecards around as you build the outline section of your Story Bible. The program also lets you save your research files in the same place as your outline and manuscript. There's a cost for the software but, if you want to keep everything in one place, consider the investment.

Wiki Software – You can find free software that will allow you to build a hypertext database for your story (similar to how Wikipedia works). Wikis allow for non-linear thinking, embedding of additional files, and internal linkage between pages. This helps to find related information quickly, and to keep your notes in one place. (Example: You can click straight from one character's history into the basic bio info on another character that plays a part in that history.) Seeing your thoughts laid out with the same authority as real-world wikis can make your world feel more legitimate, building self-confidence for you as a writer, especially when you take your file from "edit mode" and export it as html files.

This Workbook – You can write directly on the pages in this book (assuming you bought the print version) and make extra notes in the margins. But you may find yourself needing to do a worksheet for more than one character or more than one setting, so you may want to dedicate a separate notebook or computer document for overflow notes. You can also make copies of the worksheets from this book for your personal use. If you are using the e-book version of Story Like a Journalist, the instructions section for each worksheet contain a link to a printable version of that worksheet, which is to be printed for personal use only.

Story Bible Overarching Worksheet (O-1)

Use this as an organizational tool to synthesize everything you learn by working through the other worksheets. Just give the overview of each section, so you have the most important information easily at hand when (if you are a planner) you start drafting your story, or (if you are a discovery writer) when you start editing your draft. Other workbooks in this series provide additional insight and instruction for some of the elements mentioned here.

Compiling a Story Bible

At its heart, a Story Bible is just a collection of lists -- both to-dos and have-dones. The document may be in flux – but you should be building a comprehensive plan, so that when you are ready to write your novel, you have all the information you could possibly need close at hand.

Continue building it as you write and uncover new things. (I like to keep a separate "to fix" list as I write or edit.)

Character Notes

I also keep a separate list, organized by character, for bits of dialogue that feel like things the character might say that haven't yet found a spot in the story, along with fragments of scenes starring her.

Having a list of character names helps keep the names from being too similar. For instance, if you have a lot of two syllable names that all either start with c, k or s OR end with y-sounds, it gets confusing to the reader fast.

> *I'd like you to meet Cindy, Sandy, Macie, Cadie, Chloe, Cassie and Kaitlyn. Can you keep them all straight in your head?*

This also helps when you want to make sure you aren't using the same name in a different story or don't quite remember how you spelled Queekkkgleth.

Settings and Objects Notes

The same goes when you are trying to remember a place you invented or what you called the technology that makes your character's starship run. This comes in surprisingly handy if you need to find all the times a character used a technology or all the times they visited a particular place. If your character invents things, is part of a spy organization, or lives in a futuristic/fantastic society, chances are you've created a lot of these.

Named Characters List (A-2)

Keep a running list of each character name you choose. Update this list any time you add a character, change a character's name, or someone gives the character a new nickname.

Name Meaning -- Look up any real-world associations with the name to make sure it is appropriate to the character. If the name is invented, give it a meaning.

Nicknames -- Include nicknames (basically anything else – good or bad – that another character calls this character).

Role in Story – Define the character's reason for being in the story. (*Examples:* protagonist, antagonist, love interest)

Invented Objects and Places List (A-3)

Keep a running list of each object and place name you invent. Update it any time you change and object or place name or come up with new information about the object/place.

Objects

Object – Define what the object is. Look up proposed names to make sure they don't have any unexpected real-world meanings or unintended associations.

Use -- Note how you use the object in the story.

Role in Story – Note why this object is important in the story. Who uses it and why?

Places

Place -- Places can include everything from planets or countries to named businesses and schools – even your character's home, if it is a named ranch or estate. Look up proposed names to understand any similarities to real place names/other words.

History Factoid – Note what this place is known for. What major event happened here? What makes this place unique? Give us something to remember.

Role in Story – Note why this place is important. Who visits it and why?

Determining Narration

Narration is all about who is telling your story, that person's level of objectivity and her relationship to the characters the story is actually about.

Sometimes you want distance.

> -- The Sherlock Holmes stories (Sir Arthur Conan Doyle) wouldn't have been nearly as satisfying if told by Holmes himself. He's too abrasive – and too efficient. If we were in his mind, we'd have the mystery figured out in half the time, and with half the satisfaction.

> -- In *The Great Gatsby* (F Scott Fitzgerald), Gatsby isn't aware of the tragic course he's on. Without Nick there to tell us the tragic ending, and to give it context, we would have no idea what Gatsby's story really means.

Sometimes you want intimacy.

> -- *The Martian* (Andy Weir) gives us Mark's mental process as he does science to apply fairly dry concepts to form his survival plan on this barren alien planet. Which, filtered through his viewpoint, and with his life at stake, becomes fascinating.

> -- In *The Curious incident of the Dog in the Nighttime* (Mark Haddon) being inside Christopher's mind allows us to understand why a character with Asperger's syndrome is reacting in ways that wouldn't necessarily seem reasonable from the outside. And his inability to understand the context of some of the events he himself is part of is heartbreaking.

Narrators vary in their objectivity. This can be intentional, as your unreliable narrator lies to us about what the characters are really doing, or about the motivations behind those actions. Alternately, the character may simply not be self-aware enough to understand (or even think to examine) his own motivations.

Choosing a Narrator

You need to pick someone to tell your story. This is the viewpoint character. This person is not necessarily who the story is about. As in the example with Gatsby, Nick (the viewpoint character) is not the protagonist. Gatsby is.

Sometimes, the person telling the story is a narrator, sometimes a person participating in the events to some extent, sometimes the protagonist herself. This is going to make a big difference in how your novel is structured and what parts of the story get told.

Even if your story is told by multiple people, there should be one person who is most important. Just like you only get one protagonist (by definition!) whose story this is, you only get one main viewpoint character.

Frame Structures

Frame structures are pieces of narration that take place outside of the timeline of the main story. These can be prologues, epilogues, bookends (which place a separate narrative both before and after the main story), or sometimes take more experimental forms.

These are effective when they comment on the main story, and doubly so when the characters in the frame are changed by the main story.

> -- In the film version of *The Princess Bride*, Fred Savage's character's relationship with his grandfather, and to some extent his values and levels of empathy, are completely changed by the lessons he's learning from the story his grandfather is reading.

Frame Devices are also effective when they are used to give the reader a piece of information that will be needed when the story starts, especially when there is no way for the viewpoint character to know this information.

> *In Free Chocolate, I start with a prologue where my protagonist's father is killed. An astute reader will pick up on the fact that in Chapter 1, when Bo's mother shows up with her new boyfriend, mom's new guy is the man who killed Bo's father. Even though Bo doesn't know this fact, it increases the tension for the reader in a scene that is otherwise about having dinner and trying to get her mother to approve of Bo's own new boyfriend.*

Too often, though, frame devices just spill out backstory or give an overview of the worldbuilding. For this reason, they are a hard sell for many readers. So if you use one, be prepared to justify your choice.

Tense

Choosing a tense is all about determining the distance your narrator has from the story.

Present Tense -- This focuses the action and provides immediacy. This story is happening now. Right now! Which means there is much less chance for reflection or context.

Past Tense – This gives room for reflection – but you sacrifice immediacy. Depending on how the story is structured, it may give away that the character will survive the events of the story, which can reduce tension. This is less of an issue when the story is set in the recent past and told completely chronologically.

Sometimes stories are told out of order, using an experimental form of tense. This is difficult to pull off successfully. If you do attempt it, you still need a structure that builds logically, giving the same type of revelation moments and feeling that you are making progress that we would get from a chronological structure.

A variation on this, in medias res, starts with a dramatic scene, and then flashes back to the event that will eventually spark this scene. We catch up with the opening scene between half and three quarters of the way through.

Narrative Tone

You need a consistent narrative voice throughout the story. One of the most important elements for us to believe the story is being told by the same person is your narrator's tone. While you should allow for some tonal variation due to scene content, a person who is an optimist will narrate even an action scene or a scene of loss with an optimistic undertone. A lyrically-hearted person will bring a hint of poetry even to a scene involving folding laundry.

Make your choice and lean into it.

Stream of Consciousness and Deep POV

Some narration techniques go deep inside the character's psychological processes.

Stream of Consciousness – This technique focuses on perceptions. The character's feelings, thoughts and reactions are like a flowing stream washing over the reader. There may be little or no conventionally-formatted dialogue.

Deep Point of View – This technique attempts to do the same thing – but with more attention to traditional formatting. Dialogue tags from the viewpoint character are eliminated, and all narration is assumed to be the character's thoughts, but dialogue still goes in quotes.

Narration Worksheet (A-4)
Make decisions about the narrator for your manuscript. Update this worksheet if you change who the narrator(s) will be.

Choosing a Narrator -- Determine whether you will have one narrator or multiple, and what role this person will have in the story. Decide how the story will affect the narrator.

Frame Structures – Decide whether this story needs elements that add context from other points in time/points of view. As these can pull readers away from the main story when used unnecessarily, justify your yes answers.

Tense – Decide whether this narrator is telling the story in present or past tense. Determine the implications this will have on your story – past tense allows for more of the distance required to have insight on the events, present tense makes things more immediate and move faster.

Narrative Tone – Decide how you want your narrator to come across. This will affect the emotions readers feel while reading your story.

Techniques – Decide if you plan to use specific narrative techniques.

Determining Point of View

You need to decide if the character will tell the story to us as she experienced it, or if you want to create a layer of distance by referring to her in the third person.

> -- I picked up the umbrella and stepped out into the rain.

> vs.

> -- She picked up the umbrella and stepped out in the rain.

If you have more than one person telling the story, you will need to decide whether to follow each person closely, staying in his head and heart until moving on to the next person (third person limited) or to designate an all-knowing narrator to tell us what's going on in all the characters' heads.

A story is created by putting together a series of scenes (in which the character takes actions and speaks) and sequels (in which the character reflects). If you are in limited third, stick in one viewpoint character's head in a given scene/sequel pairing. Give him/her a chance to finish the psychological process before moving on to someone else.

Basically:

> *First Person* – "I" tell the story.

> *Second Person* – "You" are experiencing the story.

> *Third Person Limited* – The narrator is in "his" or "her" head.

> *Third Person Omniscient* – The all-knowing narrator is in everybody's head.

Be cautious about mixing first/third person, or having multiple first-person narrators. This can be jarring or seem amateurish. It has been done successfully, though, so don't think you absolutely can't.

> -- In *The Martian* by Andy Weir, the first half of the narration is exclusively first person from Mark's POV, then later third person POVs are added of the people trying to help him – and there's even a scene from the POV of a piece of canvas holding together his critical equipment.

Second person is difficult to work with for any story where you are not asking the reader to make choices. (Remember those old adventure books where it was like, *You reach a junction in the corridor. Do you go right or left?*) This is because you are telling us readers that we ARE something – young, old, a criminal, a mother, a florist – whatever you've defined the character as – and many of us are mentally saying, *No, I'm not*, every step of the way.

Scope and Scale

Scope – This is the amount of time and space covered in your story. A family saga that spans four generations, a journey that takes your characters half way across the universe, a huge dimension-shaping idea that the characters all find themselves wrestling with – that's a large scope.

Scale -- This is the size of the story. If you were making a film instead of writing a novel, you would be able to measure this by budget – more characters, more settings, more costumes all mean a larger scale.

Both of these factors come into play when you're deciding the point of view that's best for your story.

Third person omniscient is probably the easiest way to manage large casts of characters and sweeping settings. It is especially effective when much of the story is external to the characters' minds, and when the writing feels cinematic. You can narrate like a camera zooming in on one person's plight, then out again to give an overview of the action, then zoom in on someone else.

The more intimate your story is, and the smaller the cast, the more often first person is a good fit. First person also works for stories where a great deal of what is going on is interior to the characters. Writing in first allows you to feel like you are the character, telling your story to someone, maybe opening up about these traumatic events for the first time.

Third person limited falls somewhere in between. You get the benefits of close storytelling – being inside the character's heart and mind – with the added flexibility of being able to switch to the viewpoint of other characters. (One character per scene, please, with third person limited.) This allows you to tell a large-scope story with an intimate feel.

No narration choice is wrong, but each will limit your writing in different ways.

> -- Imagine that the original Star Wars trilogy was re-envisioned first person, from Luke's point of view. You would lose every scene he wasn't there to see – nothing on board the Death Star, nothing of Leia losing her planet. Instead, you have a much more intimate story of a son, his broken father, and the boy's replacement father figure/mentor.

Interior Life

The biggest advantage novelists have over screenwriters is our ability to explore a character's interior life. We get to share his moment-to-moment thoughts and emotions. We can describe the way he physically feels in stressful situations – from the inside.

This also allows us to plumb the character's psyche, which can contain some of the most fascinating aspects of our fictions.

But it is possible to write a story that feels cinematic, and stays predominately outside the character, with a focus more on action and external conflict.

It is difficult to explore anyone's interior life in third person omniscient. If you want to bare your character's emotions and thoughts, stick to first or close third.

External Narration

Narration – This means everything happening in your story that isn't dialogue, internal monologue, or characters moving physically and taking actions. Other models also include the movement and actions as narration.

Either way, you can provide extensive narration in third person omniscient. The ability to comment on events and give context to what is happening, or simply to say *Meanwhile, on the other side of the kingdom . . .*, is what omniscient offers that makes up for not writing from inside the character.

If you go first person, even the external narration is filtered through your character's point of view. This means your character can *suppose* the context of other peoples' actions – but she can't actually *know*.

POV Worksheet (A-5)

Make choices as to how you will handle point of view. Use the worksheet to help determine the best fit for the story you want to tell. Update the worksheet if you decide to change the way you are handling POV.

Scope – Decide how big of a cast you plan to have and how wide or narrow the scope will be.

Interior Life – Decide how much of your story will focus on your character's thoughts, emotions and interior monologue.

External Narration – Decide how much you want to focus on external narration (anything that isn't character speech/thoughts).

Plot your choices along the x and y axis in the chart. Whatever quadrant your plotted point lands in would make the most obvious choice for viewpoint for your story. You don't always have to do the expected, but consider if it would be a comfortable fit.

Setting the Rules

Having rules for your novel world is important, if you don't want readers to feel betrayed by the events in your novel. This basically comes down to setting expectations early on and sticking to them. If you're writing a cozy mystery, and suddenly your story takes on heavy levels of on-page violence, the reader is likely to put the book down and never pick up another of your stories. If you promise a romance, and the two lovers wind up calling it a day and moving to separate countries, the reader is going to throw your book across the room.

This can also be specific to the expectations you set as an individual author.

> *In an early draft of Pure Chocolate, I killed off a particular character. (Let's be honest. A lot of people die in the Chocoverse books.) But the reaction my agent had to this: absolutely not. I had presented a world where, yes bad things happen, but bad doesn't triumph or last forever. That particular character's death would have broken two of the other characters in ways that wouldn't have been easy to heal. Therefore, it would have broken the "rule" I set in the first book about the tone and level of events.*

Whatever elements you introduce in your story need to be logically possible from the beginning of the manuscript. This is especially true if you are inventing rules about the way things work in a speculative world.

Having a list can help you check back after you finish your draft to make sure things are consistent, so that you are not violating your own rules.

Why Set Rules?

It can feel like setting rules limits your creativity as a writer. After all, it's not like absolutely anything could happen anymore. You've made choices you will have to stick with and work around. But in reality, that's a powerful benefit.

Limits Create Suspense – When readers know your rules, they can start to make guesses about what might happen, and fear that your characters won't be able to extricate themselves from dangers. We like to feel like we were smart enough to see things coming.

Limits Challenge Your Characters – When characters have to work within limits, be it the rules of law that police officers have to abide by, or the drawbacks that come with the super-powers you've gifted them with, or the societal rules of your setting in Victorian England, you automatically provide obstacles for your characters to work around. It is a lot more satisfying for the character to figure out how to use three reflective surfaces to hit a target with the laser vision she's been afraid to use since she accidentally killed someone, than for her to pick up a stun gun that Big Bad just happened to drop.

Genre

For the purposes of this workbook, all fiction categories (including literary fiction, women's fiction, commercial fiction, and young adult fiction) are being termed genres. It's just simpler.

If you're not sure what genre you are writing, visit a bookstore and see where books similar to yours are shelved. Or get on Amazon and see what categories books similar to yours are filed under.

Genre expectations are going to give you some built in rules. Romances ALWAYS have to have an HEA (Happily Ever After) or an HFN (Happy Enough for Now). Category mysteries ALWAYS have to reveal who the criminal is.

Genre Codes and Conventions

Every literary genre is going to have a specific set of codes and conventions. These are what allow readers to become fans of a genre – the readers have certain expectations, and have seen those expectations met. This leaves them hungry for more.

A genre's readers expect familiar details – but are always looking for a twist. And many readers love a flipped trope. You can only give them one if you are familiar with your genre. Read widely in it, and note how other writers are employing these codes and conventions.

Codes – These refer to content expectations. A genre's common tropes, character types, and thematic discussions (romance says something about love, mystery says something about justice) are all codes. You can use this to your advantage – reader expectations allow you to use a sort of shorthand by matching the code expectation with the element in your book.

Conventions – These refer to stylistic issues. There are genre conventions for things like book length, tense, plot structure – even chapter length. These are things you especially need to pay attention to if you plan to submit your book to publishing professionals, who are looking to work with people who understand the conventions.

Safety

Certain types of characters are usually protected from violence and death. (For example, in cozy mysteries, you won't see anyone kill a cat, even if that cat has been threatened or kidnapped. Same goes for kids.) This affects how readers will attach to characters. If a particular character is safe, it is okay to become truly invested in her as a person.

If we think she might not survive the story, we will keep our emotional distance a little to protect ourselves. This is one reason why the comic relief characters and the innocents in a story (characters who are usually safe) can sometimes be more fan-favorites than the actual heroes.

Sometimes the plot structure demands that certain characters will be safe, and psychologically, readers sense that. We will attach fully to those characters.

If you want to signal that no one in the story is safe (which means that we have no right later to feel betrayed, no matter who dies), you can kill or injure a traditionally safe character early on in the narrative.

Intensity

The intensity of violence or romance needs to be signaled early on in your book, so that readers will not become invested in your plot, only to realize half way through that this is NOT the book they expected or wanted. (Too little intensity can be just as disappointing as too much intensity – it is all about expectation.)

This doesn't mean that if the overall violence level is high you have to have a murder on the first page – but we should see characters carrying weapons or discussing violence in the opening chapters.

Some sub-genres have built-in intensity levels. For instance, contrast a cozy mystery with noir.

Ease

Readers will want to know how hard it is for characters to do things in your world. We need context too. If your character can bring rain in a drought, through either technology or superpowers, is he the most-sought-after person on the planet or is he more like a plumber?

Think about mystery novels. How hard was it for the bad guy to commit the murder? If the method required high physical skill, or specialized knowledge, this limits the pool of suspects. And understanding that lets us feel like we are in on solving the crime. Readers want a similar feeling, no matter what the genre.

You can use history (real or imagined) to shape your character's ability to act and the ease in which she can travel and communicate.

> -- How long did it really take to get from Rome to Carthage on foot? On horseback?

> -- What would your protag have to do to get a message to her parents after emigrating to "The Colonies?"

Some common technologies that have to be addressed if they show up in your book:

Space Travel -- Is it as easy as taking an airplane? Or is it a one-way trip that may take more than one generation?

Time Travel -- Can you kill your own grandpa? Or are you a viewer who cannot interact with anyone? Somewhere in between?

Teleportation -- Is this technology safe? What is the percent rate of not coming out the other side? Are you guaranteed to show up in the right place?

Setting Rules for Your World Worksheet (A-6)

Determine the basic rules of your world. Update this sheet when you add new implications about the rules you have set or add new rules that come out of plot events.

Genre -- Determine your genre. Sometimes a story could fall into different genres depending on how it is written (for instance, a summer travel story could be women's fiction, literary fiction, or category romance).

Genre Codes and Conventions – Decide what tropes, plot devices, standards, etc. from your genre you want to embrace. Also note tropes you would like to flip or comment on.

Safety – Decide which types of characters are safe in your world. Think how you will subtly cue to readers early on which types of characters are NOT safe.

Intensity – Decide how intense you want the reading experience to be. Think how you will subtly cue to readers early on what kind of ride they are about to take.

Real-Word Influence – Decide if the rest of the rules for your world will come from how the real-world works. If you have invented a speculative world, outline how that speculative world works using the additional worksheet pages.

Example:

>*Point 1:* On planet Giantantia, corrosive rain falls every day. Because of this:
>
>A. The giant ants that live there have developed body armor that is even stronger than their natural exoskeletons.
>
>B. Humans visiting the planet have to find shelter during the rainstorm, or die horribly.
>
>C. Plants that absorb water during the rainstorm are toxic to humans, but not to giant ants, who have a way to neutralize the toxins.
>
>D. Metal (such as space ships) left out in this rain will develop holes rather quickly.

Determining Ease Worksheet (A-7)

Determine how easy it is for characters to accomplish different things in your story's setting. Update if you make significant changes to the setting.

Write out answers to the questions, considering how technology is used/viewed in this story world.

Circle anything that feels like it could be used as a plot point or complication.

Making Promises

The elements you introduce in the early part of your manuscript become promises you make to the reader about the type of story you are going to deliver. For example, if your protagonist draws a gun in the first chapter, you promise a story that will have violence.

Interestingly, these promises relate back to the journalist's ideas about the lede – and about the 5-Ws and H.

A journalist's lede contains everything you need to know to get into the rest of the story, and gives the reader an exciting entry point. (See the Novelist's Lede Worksheet later in this chapter). Your novel's hook does the same thing. But you can't hook a reader into one novel (promising a coming of age story with nostalgia and romance) and deliver a different one (about becoming a soccer star and taking the competition DOWWWWN). This is why novels that start with dream sequences or simulations rarely work: it is a bait and switch tactic that turns off many readers.

Avoid gimmicks and instead promise us:

WHO – a specific character we can follow through the story as he grows and changes.

WHAT – a problem that teases the central conflict. It doesn't have to directly introduce the bad guys, but it should foreshadow either the external conflict to come, or highlight the character's internal struggle that will cause her to arc.

WHEN – a setting that allows us to be in a specific time period. This influences the tone and mood of the book and slipping away from the feel of the time period is one of the easiest promises to break.

WHERE – a complete, immersive story world. Whether it is contemporary New York, 16th Century China or a colony on Alpha Centauri, we need to believe that we are there.

HOW – a plot question. This is another easy promise to break – you start by asking one plot question (how can Mia and Raj escape the rampaging dinosaurs taking over their school?) and at the climax, answer a different one (how did

Mia and Raj's love overcome Mia's jealousy and Raj's sister's interference). Leaving the reader wondering about the remaining rampaging dinosaurs.

WHY – a sense of meaning to your story. You're promising that reading your novel will be worth our time, that you're going somewhere with this.

In addition to these basic promises, each individual story makes specific promises to follow up on characters and plotlines introduced. You're asking us to trust you when you tell us certain things are important. If you introducing something with an intriguing question attached, or if you bring it up more than once, we're going to expect you to follow up. Otherwise we will stop trusting you and stop caring.

Your additional promises should be relevant to the main story in some way. If you ask an intriguing question about one of the characters or an element of your setting early on in the story, the answer needs to play into solving the plot problem, even if indirectly. If you introduce a subplot, that subplot needs to comment thematically on the main plot, or smash into the main plot in a way that changes things significantly.

Don't Clutter Your Story with Promises

Every promise that you make will increase your novel's word count significantly, as you have to follow up with the new characters we will have to meet, the subplot just unleashed, or the MacGuffin we have to watch your characters chase. Make too many promises, and you'll wind up with an unwieldly manuscript that's far too long for the current marketplace.

Plus, if you give us too many things to care about, we won't know what's important. The traditional writing principle of **Chekhov's Gun** is basically this: don't have a character wave a gun in the first chapter if, during the course of the story, no one is going to fire it. It doesn't have to be fired by the character we expect. Nor does it have to kill anybody. We enjoy it when promises are fulfilled in a surprising way. But it does need to impact the plot.

> *If you are writing multiple books in a series, promises that won't be addressed until a later book may need to be left out of the first one. In the Chocoverse, I wanted to introduce HGB's CEO in the second book, because he was going to be an important character in the third one. However, his presence didn't really serve a purpose in the second book's plot. I wound up removing those scenes, because they distracted from the Book 2 plotline.*

Be deliberate in the way you introduce each promise. When the idea of something important is planted in a way that is seemingly a throwaway it becomes the opposite of the "too many coincidences" syndrome. When it comes back up later, it becomes part of what makes your ending "surprising yet inevitable."

Also be deliberate if you choose to leave unfired guns on the wall. These plot elements can be distractions, red herrings, or misdirection. But use this technique with caution.

Promises to the Reader Worksheet (A-8)
Lay out the promises you are making in your story. Update this sheet when you change an aspect of what the story is about, or you add a new promise.

Your 5-Ws Promises -- Lay out your basic 5Ws that you are promising your reader. What is this story really about? The reader should know within the first couple of chapters. They should have an inkling on the first page.

Additional Promises -- Look at each additional promise you plan to introduce into the story, and how those promises will relate to the main 5-Ws that your story is about. Determine the payoff of that promise. Use the check boxes to consider how making those promises will impact the completed manuscript.

Example:

> *Promise:* We will find out who the main character's mother really is.
>
> *How is it relevant*: The protagonist (WHO) needs self-confidence to solve the plot problem (WHAT) and feels inferior not knowing where she is from.
>
> *Payoff:* The character discovers that her mother is a former alcoholic who has gotten her life back together and has been a regular at the coffee shop where the character works for several years without having the nerve to reveal who she is.

Determine if you can you keep all your promises, without diluting your story's arc or making the manuscript too long. Use the worksheet ranking to detail which of the promises you are making are most important to you. Structure your novel to make sure you have time to follow up on those without rushing.

Lessons from the Journalism Classroom

There are a number of basic lessons journalists learn in class that can benefit the novelist in terms of mind-set as well. You just have to reframe the lessons inside the novel's structure.

Be Clear and Unbiased

It is easy to think that, because you are writing fiction, there's no wrong way to do it. In one sense that is true. You are making art. You can do whatever you want. But. There is such a thing as emotional and literal truth. Stories can read as authentic – and touch people's hearts, maybe stick with them for life. Or – when authenticity is violated – stories can intentionally present a skewed view of the world and reinforce negative stereotypes.

There is a reason inauthenticity is highly frowned on in journalism. Words can damage people.

If you want to be unbiased, you need to give all if your major characters agency (the ability to be themselves, and to make choices that affect the plot's outcome.) You have to show them all respect. Don't bully or railroad characters (giving them such limited choices that they can't impact anything substantial) and don't let them be straw men (characters just designed to show how silly an opposing viewpoint is). It may be odd to think about ethical storytelling in fiction – but if you want to write respectable work, you need to let characters have their own voices and be real – even when you don't agree with them.

Agency is what allows us to feel that the character is a flesh-and-blood person with a life extending beyond the events of the story. Readers need that illusion in order to achieve and maintain empathy. We can't feel empathy for a chess piece being moved about without choice. We CAN feel empathy if that chess piece takes one look at the knight headed for his square and runs for the edge of the board.

Basically, you're giving the character free will. Real people fight hard if their ability to make choices is taken away. Your characters should do the same. We also cannot care about characters that don't care enough about their own stories to fight for what they want.

If you take away agency from your protagonist (such as having him kidnapped) the character needs to find a different kind of agency (such as fighting his captors in order to escape, getting information in the process). If he just sits around waiting for rescue, he's not actually your protagonist. The same goes for your antagonist. After all, these are the two characters whose push and pull of decision making build your plot.

Strategically limiting your protagonist's agency (take away her badge, or her driver's license), on the other hand, can force her to rely on other people, or to develop new skill sets, in ways she never imagined. If this reduction of agency happens at the beginning of a story, it can give us sympathy for her – which some protagonists sorely need.

Whatever help she accepts along the way, there is one decision she HAS to make on her own. She has to choose to face the antagonist at the climax. And she has to exercise agency in building the plan to defeat her foe.

> *In my Chocoverse books, it would have been easy to have a traditional action hero as my protagonist. There are plenty of those in the 'verse – and several of them are major characters. But the character who solves the plot problem is Bo, failed telenovela star turned culinary arts student. It is her skillset (involving diplomacy and relationship-building) that allows her to be the only one who could solve the problem without getting Earth destroyed. Therefore, the plot had to be shaped so that her skillset is what is needed to protag throughout. She leaves much of the action stuff to her friends (she is a terrible fighter), but she is the one solving the big puzzles and making the decisions that count most.*

Who Has Agency Worksheet (A-9)

Determine how the characters in your story are showing agency. Update this sheet when you add new plot elements that allow the characters to make more choices.

Character -- Make a list of your major characters. Don't worry about the barista who hands your character a cup of coffee in one scene. But each character who has a name and a viewpoint should be making significant decisions.

Meaningful Choices -- List the three most important decisions each character makes in your story. Review the list to ensure that these are actually choices (that the character could have viably made another decision) and that these actions have a measurable impact on the outcome of your story.

Do Your Research

If your story has a real-world setting, research, research, research. If your fiction deals with real-world issues or people, get multiple perspectives. If there's science or history, double-check your facts.

-- If you're writing historical fiction, some of your readers are going to know a great deal about your time period, and they will call you on shoddy research. Check dates on every piece of technology you introduce -- flashlights, bicycles, egg timers -- to make sure they would have been around in the year (not just the general period) in question.

-- Be careful when introducing real-world historical people into your fiction. There is a lot more biographical information on historic figures out there than what you're going to find in Wikipedia, and readers are going to have opinions on how this person would/would not act. Do your best to get it right, and develop a thick skin for your critics.

-- Sci-fi fans will be thrown out of the story if they repeatedly find themselves saying, "That's not how science works." Research the current literature on the topic, and then if you still have questions, consult an expert.

-- Readers who are from/live in the places you are using as your contemporary setting will know if you are getting things right – from the way people talk and what they eat, to whether Broadway is a one-way street. You owe it to them to get it right.

For historic research, large city/academic libraries will often have a special collections department. Which means there may be a library somewhere in this grouping of institutions which specializes in your time period/geographic area/topic. If so, make friends with these librarians, either in person or on-line. If it is local, take the time to visit the archive. Note: you will probably not be allowed to bring in bags/purses or pens, and may have to wear gloves to handle documents.

Art museums often have libraries attached, as do botanical research centers and university science and engineering departments. And subject experts themselves, from research scientists to chefs, are often happy to talk about their expertise if approached in a professional manner.

Less formal resources are also helpful. For instance, YouTube is a rich source of videos on how to do almost anything, and will show you what life is like in many areas of the globe.

You Don't Know What You Don't Know

When you start researching, you have to figure out what you need to know. And that can be difficult, because sometimes you don't know what there is to understand about a topic. In that case, do some general research first, to figure out what you don't know about the topic.

There's a balance to strike between researching specific questions you already know you need answers to, embracing serendipitous connections you uncover (that send your story in new directions), and stopping researching to actually start writing the novel.

Research Questions Worksheet (A-10)

Identify your potential research areas. Update this sheet as you uncover other topics you need to research.

Answer the questions to determine what research you will need to do in some of the most common categories.

Then check the boxes for general topics that might come up in your book. Use the lines to add notes on specific topics under those general headings.

Verify Your Sources

Never rely on second-hand information. This means going beyond what you think you know from reading other fiction, or from the movies. You never know what the writers/directors streamlined, simplified or changed from historical/scientific fact in order to get their stories to work. And if the writer you are using as a source also didn't do deeper research, you are in danger of passing on information that is downright wrong.

It is easier now than it would have been pre-Internet to get things right. Get to know experts, librarians and re-enactors. YouTube videos can show you how physics, weapons, art techniques, etc. really work.

Be picky about where you get your information. Commercial web sites can contain biased information (they are, after all, trying to sell you on something). And a Wikipedia entry can be edited by anyone. Web sites that have .org and .edu extensions are probably better bets. (Though the bibliography in a Wikipedia article may make a good list to start looking for legitimate sources.)

Journalists often interview subject experts, or people who were involved in the events they are writing about. You can do the same, if you approach people professionally and let them know why you want the information. Be sure to organize that person's contact information together with your notes in case you have more questions.

If your novel requires significant research, you may wish to build a bibliography as you write. (A bibliography is a list of resources consulted during the writing.)

While novelists are not usually required to turn in a bibliography with their work, it is useful to have the information at hand if your copyeditor has a question – or if you want to look at the source again. There are a small number of publishers that require bibliographies. So if you are writing in a research-heavy genre, check publisher guidelines before you start working.

Bibliography Worksheet (A-11)
Keep a running list of the sources you have used for research. Use the citation format below. If the publisher needs a bibliography (this is rare), use the publisher's suggested format instead.

Add additional sheets as you continue researching.

For print resources, list:
The author's name
The title of the publication (and the title of the article if it is an article)
The date of publication
The publishing company (for books)
The volume number (for magazines)
The page number(s)

For web resources, list:
The author's name
The title of the web page
The company or organization who owns the webpage
The web address for the page
The last date you looked at the page

For people interviewed, list:
The person's name
The date of the interview
The location of the interview
The person's contact information

Key information -- Add the key piece of information you pulled from the source. If you pull a number of different things from the same source, just keep one citation, with a reference noting where you are putting your list of additional information.

Notes -- Add any additional notes about where you found the source, other publications that relate to the source, other material the author has written, or anything else you find interesting.

Mine the Real World for Story Ideas

Have you ever heard or read a news story and thought, *That's not the real story*, or even better, *That's not the WHOLE story*? If there's something compelling enough about a particular news item that it sticks with you days later, it might just make a good basis for a novel plot.

The world around you is full of stories, whether they're being reported on the news or not. Listen to the stories people tell about their lives. Pay attention to the biographies people share on sports shows and reality television competitions.

Of course, you'll have to use your imagination to make your book different enough from the actual facts that you won't upset real people. Change the names. Set it somewhere else. Even change the genre.

> -- Say you saw a news item about a kidnapping case with an eccentric old lady who wound up with Stockholm Syndrome and didn't want to go back to the family she felt was neglecting her. --- Maybe set it in the Napoleonic Era, in the midst of the Revolution, and have her captured by someone in desperate need of the ransom money.

> -- Say you saw a reality television show about people competing to sell the most food in various cities, from their food trucks. – Maybe reframe this competition into a romance between two of the competitors.

> -- Say you saw a news item about a missing teenager. – Maybe have that teen go missing in a domed colony city on an alien planet. Because – how? Where would she have gone?

Sometimes you can use an idea from the real word in your work in-progress, by taking one element – maybe even just a character occupation – that will add something unexpected to your manuscript.

You can also mine your own life for ideas. If you have experienced loss, you can write about it with emotional authenticity. The character doesn't have to be you. Or to have experienced the same kind of loss. Give it some distance from the events that actually happened, to make it fiction.

Other Places to Look for Story Ideas

You can also look to your genre for story ideas. Considering the types of stories people tell when writing literary fiction, or portal fantasies, or romance can help spark your own unique take.

Think about the movies you like to watch, other books you like to read. Does that give you ideas for stories you might want to tell? Your Netflix watch history may well spark your imagination.

You don't want to completely rip off someone else's ideas, and you certainly don't want to re-create their story (this falls in the range between uninspired and downright plagiarism). You're just looking for inspiration.

Don't limit yourself, even if you think some people might find the idea silly. After all, someone came up with the subject of, *Tornado full of sharks*. And that turned into the six-film *Sharknado* franchise.

Besides, you never know how one idea could spark another, better idea. And if you're going to keep writing stories, your idea list will come in handy to build off of later.

Real World Story Ideas List (A-12)

Make a list of story ideas using character and plot elements that have been pulled from the news. Update as you see news stories that spark your imagination.

Add in items from bits of story that you have observed in real life. Then add ideas sparked by other fiction you have watched and read.

Circle any that you can incorporate into your current project.

Idea Generation Worksheet (A-13)

Generate ideas for your story to center on. Update this worksheet when you have a new idea, or want to brainstorm more ideas.

Idea Lists -- Examine the list of common broad topics for the genre you want to write.

Notes Page -- Write down ideas that these topics spark for specific characters and story directions. Look at the lists for other genres and see if they spark ideas for subplots, or other ways to blend stories, and make additional notes. Look for ways to incorporate ideas from the Real-World Story Ideas List.

Circle the ideas you are most interested in working with.

Define Your Angle

Your book needs to be about something specific. And it needs to stand out from other books that are about the same thing.

What makes your take on the topic/genre different from the other novels that have been written in a similar vein? This is your angle. Which in a novel, influences the theme, focus and viewpoint choices you make. It also determines the novel's tone.

Is your angle centered around a different type of character? Something unusual about the world? A different point you are trying to make? Whatever you choose, you need to be consistent and lean into it.

Genre as Conversation

Every genre (including literary fiction and women's fiction) has tropes and audience expectations that have been built up over time. These form the conversation of the genre. For example, every romance novel says something about love. Modern romance novels say something different about priorities in life and within love than romances from fifty years ago. The best modern romances build unique relationships that add something new or unexpected to the conversation on what love really means and what role it should play in the character's sense of self. Readers are looking for that "something new" in a book that still meets their genre expectations.

> -- Say you are writing a romance where two people who feared lives of paired loneliness find deep, passionate love in an arranged marriage. You need to know what current/past romance novels have said about arranged marriages before you can subtly tell publishing professionals/potential readers how your book fits.

You can stand out by determining how you want to add to that conversation, and what qualities about your writing will appeal to fans of the genre – and then playing to those strengths.

Mashups

Another way to get something new is to combine elements from different genres, creating mashups. This is how you get monster movies set in space.

Think about ways to combine things you like to read. A thriller set in a fantasy kingdom? A heist taking place in the middle of London's Great Plague? A woman's journey of self-discovery and growth through a trip to a resort on an alien planet?

Nothing is out of bounds.

> -- If you like independent female characters and mysteries and stories set in Scotland, you've got a lot of the elements for a fun police procedural.

> -- If you also like science fiction stories, give it a twist and have the murderer be a time traveler.

> -- Or set it in the future, and have your female detective be an alien who's second generation on Earth, struggling with a disconnect from her home culture.

> -- If you already had a book idea, incorporate these elements more subtly. If your original idea was for a coming of age story, develop a subplot involving a light mystery, surrounding the theft of jewelry, or around some character's secret identity.

Or you can take a familiar story and add an element. The Hollywood example always starts with *Die Hard*. So, *Die Hard* on a bus becomes *Speed*, *Die Hard* on a boat becomes *Under Siege*. I like to think how to make things lighthearted, so I propose *Die Hard* with a kid protag becomes *Home Alone*.

Don't be afraid to reimagine a basic structure that works. It doesn't mean what you come up with will feel derivative. *Die Hard* = jaded outsider/underdog defends innocents. This is also *The Seven Samurai*, *A Bug's Life*, *The Three Amigos* (substitute clueless for jaded), *The Magnificent 7*, *Shane* and *Galaxy Quest* . . . among others. Each of these films brings something new to the table.

Angle Worksheet (A-14)

Determine what will make your book stand out from others that are similar. Update this list when you add new elements to your novel.

Comp Titles -- Make a list of eight published books similar to yours.

Uniqueness -- Then fill in as many of the spaces as you can that show how your books is different. Pick the strongest one or two and focus in on those as your angle.

Genre Conversation Worksheet (A-15)
Determine how your novel will add to your genre's conversation. Update this worksheet if you change any major aspect of your book.

Research what your genre has said about your book's topic in the past and what other writers are currently saying, and then write a summary of your findings.

Look at how you want to build on or re-interpret your genre's conversation. Don't forget the things you love about your genre – write out the elements of what your genre has already said that you want to hold onto.

Idea Mashups Worksheet (A-16)
Consider ways to recombine story elements you like to create something new. Update this list when you come up with additional ideas.

5 Elements -- Make lists of what you like to read and why, to discover elements you might want to add to your story.

Mashups -- Experiment with mashing those ideas together in different ways to see if you can create a unique story idea. If you already have an idea for your manuscript, try mashing some of your favorite elements from the worksheets into it to add depth/unique elements to your original idea.

Circle the ideas you find most intriguing.

Don't Bury the Lede

Fiction never needs a summary or introduction before getting right into the story. Start with something exciting – potentially the most exciting thing about the book. Journalists call this the lede. Novelists usually refer to it as the hook. You don't have to give everything away to hook a reader. But it needs to give us a small version of your main topic or conflict (Your 5Ws) that tells the reader the essence of what your story is. If your book is about rampaging dinosaurs taking over a high school, you need to at least HINT that dinosaurs exist in your world, or that something horrible could easily happen at this high school from page one.

Back when newspapers were exclusively print, when a reporter turned in a story, the bottom few inches worth of content might get trimmed to make room for an advertisement or for breaking news. So the most important information had to come first. In your novel, don't hold back too long on important reveals and cool stuff. Even if your opening hooks us, you have to keep us engaged with the story throughout. These days, readers tend to DNF any book that doesn't give them a frequent incentive to keep reading. Which is much the same as cutting your story before it gets to the good part.

At the same time, don't infodump (which amounts to burying the lede under a mountain of revelations and facts). Keep your narrative moving.

Of the seven types of ledes traditionally identified for journalists, three of them involve telling stories (antidotal, observation/commentary on a scenario, and personal experience). The others are: starting with a startling statement (a zinger), setting the scene, asking a question, or just stating the topic. There is something to be learned from considering each of these in terms of fiction. You HAVE to be telling a story on page 1, but can you incorporate one of these other techniques? Startle your readers with your novel's first sentence. Make what happens next such a compelling question that they have to read on.

Novelist's Lede Worksheet (A-17)
Try re-writing your novel's opening (your lede/initial hook) using different focus points. Add additional sheets if you need more space to write.

These prompts consider the different standard approaches used to draw people into a news story. Try to make your novel "newsworthy."

Determine which approach is the most effective for the story you are trying to tell.

Write Straightforward Sentences and Scenes
Write to communicate, not to impress. If you get too flowery, with overly complex structure, you slow the pace of your story. This can quickly lose you readers. Even if you are writing for artistic effect, clarity needs to trump cleverness.

Similarly, try not to overuse obscure words, jargon, or acronyms. If you do use them, explain what the word means the first time you use it. (See the Jargon Worksheet later in this chapter) Anything that makes a reader stop and puzzle something out will slow the pace of your story.

Some stories may naturally move more slowly, and some voices will be poetic, but this needs to feel coherent and consistent.

Physicality

What readers remember about your characters is usually not based on their physical features. We read (as opposed to watching video) to get inside the characters' minds, to see them for who they are when adversity had burned them raw and laid them bare. BUT. Without physicality – the sense that the character has a specific body and physical appearance and is in fact moving through space – we cannot cast the illusion on our own minds that this character is a real person. This is a problem, because we cannot empathize with abstract constructs.

Part of writing straightforward scenes is including the character's physicality in the scene. And this means including the five senses – plus the kinetic sense that characters feel when moving through space or experiencing equilibrium shifts. It is easy to describe what a character (or your omniscient narrator) sees, just like with a movie. But you get more oomph when you include the other senses.

Imagine you are writing a fight scene. Can the character hear the sounds of bone breaking? What about the scent of fear or the taste of sweat? And here's what kicks it up a couple of notches: Can you capture a sense what adrenaline is doing to the viewpoint character's body and mind?

Put the reader in the scene, and we will remember the thematic point you were trying to make more viscerally than any amount of speeches or statistics. This is why journalists use story elements in the first place. And as a novelist, you owe it to us to keep us immersed in the story.

Imagery

Imagery is what gives your story physicality. This is where you use language to represent objects, actions, and ideas. Done right, this will light up the same part of the reader's brain as if we were actually engaging in the action instead of your character.

According to many models, there are 7 types of imagery (though other models may subdivide them into roughly 20). These include:

Visual Imagery -- what the character sees, including graphics and pictures.

Auditory Imagery – what the character hears, including dialogue, background noise, and music. (May be written as onomatopoeia, where the words sound like the action being described.)

Olfactory Imagery – what the character smells, including negative odors, pleasant scents, and familiar smells that may trigger involuntary autobiographical memory.

Gustatory Imagery – what the character can taste, including the flavors of food and impurities in the air.

Tactile Imagery -- what the character senses in terms of touch, including physical textures.

Kinesthetic Imagery – the character's sense of bodily motion.

Organic Imagery – a character's experiences inside their physical body, including pain, fatigue and hunger. Sometimes also includes emotion. Can be referred to as subjective imagery.

Body Language

Another important aspect of physicality is body language. A character's body movements and facial expressions are a big clue for the audience to gauge your character's emotions. If the character's body language is at odds with the character's words, we are going to believe the body language. You can use that strategically to imply subtext to dialogue, or to imply that a character is lying.

Body language hits all the empathy circuits in a reader's brain, because it is universal, and the brain processes it more viscerally than speech. If you can't imagine what your character's habitual body language is like, you may need to get to know her better.

Blocking

Blocking is important for us to be able to follow the action in a scene.

If you were making a film, your blocking would be how you arrange all the actors in relation to the camera, and how you have them move through the scene. Novelists do the same thing – in their imaginations.

But sometimes it can be hard to visualize this. Or you may have a hard time translating what is in your imagination onto the page in a way that seems physically plausible. It can help to sketch the scene, or set up objects to represent things in the scene. Once you see things in motion, you can describe it much more easily.

Storyboarding

Storyboarding is a similar technique, also borrowed from film. This is where you sketch out important scenes so you can develop the aesthetic of the piece. This can help you discover what is important about your setting, the key ways in which your characters move, or the real mood of your story.

Try sketching different aspects of your story any time you feel stuck, because sometimes changing to a different medium can unblock you.

Imagery Worksheet (A-18)

Consider a scene that you plan on putting in your story. If possible, find a picture or YouTube video that reminds you of the scene.

Freeze the world around your character for a moment in the middle of this scene. Imagine that the character can look around and really experience all the details of the immediate environment.

Chart -- Fill out the chart from your character's point of view. Really get into the sensory elements.

Paragraph -- Write a paragraph including at least four of the seven sensory inputs. Try to use the descriptive words to imply how the character feels emotionally about the scene without directly stating it.

Repeat this exercise any time a scene feels flat, or where you can't quite figure out what a character is feeling.

Body Language Observation Worksheet (A-19)

Visit a public place and sit, quietly, people watching. Observe ten people who display different body language.

Body Language – For each person you observe, record 3 visual descriptors of the body language and list the emotion those descriptors add up to. Circle the 3 body language/emotion sets that most intrigue you.

In-Story Body Language -- Then assign this body language to a character in your story. Write a couple of sentences incorporating these descriptors, and see if it feels right for the character.

Example:

> *Body Language:* Hunched shoulders, no eye contact, crossed arms = nervous
>
> *In-Story Body Language:* Sunny didn't look at any of the other contestants as she made her way onto the stage. She pulled her hunched shoulders back down to where they belonged as she approached the microphone. She managed to make eye contact with Mrs. Martinez, the friendly music instructor who had come out to adjust her microphone. Mrs. Martinez smiled as she lowered the silver stand. "Don't cross your arms, mija."

Repeat this exercise any time you need to connect to a character's feelings and core attributes.

Blocking Worksheet (A-20)

Imagine your story is playing out on a stage. Pretend you are viewing this from above. Sketch where your characters are in relation to each other. Also mark important elements, such as any objects the characters are trying to obtain, any weapons in play and any obstacles.

Alternately, if you need to block an action scene, you can use board game pieces or small tokens to keep track of how your characters are moving in relation to each other.

Repeat this exercise any time you have a scene you can't visualize.

Storyboarding Worksheet (A-21)

Work out the important action in a scene or series of scenes.

Boxes – Sketch the important elements of the scene opening in the first box, then sketch how the scene changes as it progresses in the remaining boxes.

Lines – Use the lines to brainstorm key phrases that come from the images you drew. Incorporate these phrases when you write the scene/scenes.

Repeat this exercise any time you want to track the progress of a scene/set of scenes. You can also use it to sketch your main plot points for the entire novel.

Use Quotes

Journalists use quotes. Novelists do too – only you get to call it dialogue. Capturing the actual words a character says adds umph to the scene and lets the reader into the character's mindset and opinions in a way that summary can't. Characters are just abstract ideas until they start to walk and talk. Then suddenly they become real people.

Dialogue can help your third-person narrator maintain the role of an outside observer, while giving the viewpoints of multiple characters. The narrator is just recording what each individual has said.

In the first person, dialogue helps keep your narrator's voice distinct from the other characters.

Consider giving characters a catchphrase (a word or set of words the character uses multiple times in the course of the story). This helps us remember which character is speaking. Your character should not be using his catchphrases every time he opens his mouth, though, or we will find it annoying, real fast.

You can also build a more extensive set of words that that character is allowed to use – and that no one else can. This will make his manner of speaking feel unique. Your characters are specific people. This should come across in the way they speak. Different characters are going to use different words for the same objects based on their background and personality. Everyone in your story deserves their own dialogue tics. Having a handy list of these divided by character saves time looking back for how they said something last time.

Determining Linguistics

How do people speak in your story world? Things like slang, mindset, and topics of polite conversation can be defined for a society or subculture, as well as for individuals.

Language is used differently in societies where people read and write, versus those where all communication has to be conveyed from memory. If you invented a society where telepathy was a common means of communication, that society might not even have sentence structure as we know it.

Linguistics can also provide insight into the dynamics of a society if there is a language used only by certain classes of people (a dead language used only by academics, a pidgin dialect used only by people from a certain area) or is only legal to use in certain contexts.

Lexicons and Glossaries

Lists of how you are using language in your story can be helpful, especially if you are setting your book in a different time or place. Unfamiliar words, whether they are from a different time period or words you invent, will need to function like foreign language in your story. You will need to teach the reader how to use them. The more invented language you include, the more "foreign words" the reader will have to learn. Once we grasp the terms, though, it will feel natural for characters to keep using them.

Glossaries – These are lists of terms and definitions. Use them for words relating to a specific topic or way of speaking. If you are building a glossary for slang in your world, remember to include words for both positive and negative concepts. If you design the slang to have a sense of cohesion, understanding one word helps with understanding the rest.

Lexicons -- A lexicon is more extensive. It covers the entire vocabulary of a language. This may be useful for cataloging words relating to your book's culture, and also words borrowed from other cultures, and from real-world occupations. If your protag's a pirate captain, a list of actual nautical terms may be helpful. If the story's set in ancient Greece, you may need a smattering of period-appropriate Greek words.

Lexicons can be used as inspirations for the slang that would arise in that culture (*Example:* What would your pirate captain call a make of boat known to leak? Can it be a play on the official name?) Keep a running list of words that could be unusual euphemisms for the uncomfortable topics in your world. Keep track of which words are considered extremely polite and those considered offensive, so you can put them into the mouths of appropriate characters.

If you are working with English or writing in another real-world language, look to the thesaurus for more interesting ways to say things. Also record bits of overheard dialogue that could be a good fit for the world.

Languages tend to borrow words and concepts from each other, especially if the groups speaking it are in close proximity, or are able to communicate electronically with ease. If you are writing a real-world setting, think about how the various language groups living in that place influence each other's speech.

You can do the same when inventing settings. If there is more than one race/group in your fantastic world, communication between all your characters can be a complex issue. You can handle it in a number of ways:

> -- You can have characters that don't understand each other. They can mime concepts, draw pictures – and have large numbers of miscommunications.

> -- You can have a "lingua franca," favored commercial language, or pidgin that most races can use to speak to each other.

> -- You can have a device that translates universally (think the babel fish from Hitchhiker's Guide).

Jargon

Using jargon can mark a character as part of an in group. Done right, judicious use of jargon can also make the reader feel like part of that in group. The key is introducing each new word, phrase or acronym in a way where it is defined by context, or giving a definition for the word unobtrusively in the narration. This is very similar to using foreign language in your writing. You want to honor the people who speak it – but you have to teach readers who don't know the vocabulary everything we will need to follow along.

Too much jargon can slow the pace of your story, so consider having someone who doesn't know this in group's vocabulary take a look at your work and give feedback.

Constructing Dialogue

Dialogue needs to be specific to the character. It should be based on the character's psychological disposition, age, geographic background, educational background, hobbies, occupations and social class.

Even if characters are similar in their backgrounds, you can vary their dialogue based on how they relate to language. Is this the kind of character who thinks before she speaks? Or one who would rather observe his surroundings and answers in monosyllables when pressed? Or one who just wants to be the center of attention and will keep talking as long as you let her?

You can also vary it based on how characters emotionally react to situations. If the character is embarrassed, does he get defensive? Or does she laugh it off? Or does he apologize, not just then but repeatedly?

Language Overview Worksheet (A-22)
Determine how language will be used in your story world. Update this worksheet if you make significant changes to your setting.

Consider the languages spoken in the area, and also how the characters interact with language in general (including education and literacy rates).

Circle anything that feels like it could be used for a plot point or a complication.

Lexicon Worksheet (A-23)
Determine the basics of an invented language in your story world. Skip this worksheet if your story uses a real-world setting. Update this worksheet as you come up with new vocabulary and language rules as you write.

Syntax – Make basic decisions about the syntax rules the language will follow. Then write out notes on additional rules for the language.

Mindset – Consider the cultural mindset of the society, and how that impacts the language use.

Vocabulary – Start building a vocabulary/word meaning list.

Try to tailor these lists to include words/concepts relevant to your story.

Jargon Worksheet (A-24)

Determine how jargon will be used by characters in your story world. Update this worksheet as you come across the need for new vocabulary as you write.

Research to learn how jargon is used in the real-world occupation, hobby or social group your character is a fictional part of. Then write out some of the words, acronyms and phrases your character might need to use in your story. Also jot down the exact meaning of the word/phrase/acronym.

Circle any words/phrases that spark ideas for plot points or complications.

Word Choice Chart (A-25)

Determine what words different characters use for common concepts based on who they are. Add to this worksheet when you need to determine how different characters would discuss a specific concept.

Identity Blocks -- List or create three different characters who could appear in your story. Try to make them different as far as geographic/cultural background and occupation. It is also easier to tell characters apart if they have different temperaments.

Generic vs Specific Words -- In the left column, list generic words that are relevant to your plot. Fill in how each character would use a different specific word for that generic concept in their dialogue.

Examples:

	Character 1	Character 2	Character 3
Canine	doggo	mutt	pupper
Carbonated Beverage	soda	Coke	pop
House	the hacienda	home	my place

Story Bible Overarching Worksheet

Overview

Premise

Write a premise for your story. This is a concise statement of what the story is about, including WHO your characters is, WHAT they have to do in the story, WHAT goal stands in their way, and WHY they have to achieve it. Refer to it to keep you on track as you work. Does everything in your outline support this statement? Is your protagonist the one solving the problems? If the answer is no, revise your outline, or change this "thesis" statement.)

_____

_____

_____

_____

_____

_____

Theme

(Consider the meaning you want the reader to take away from your story. Write out the primary theme to keep you on track as you work – do your plot events and character arcs work together to make the artistic statement you intended?)

_____

_____

_____

_____

_____

Stakes
(Write out your protagonist's personal, public, and ultimate stakes. This is what your character stands to lose if they don't achieve the plot goal, on a personal level, on an external plot level, and on a human level. The stakes should get more intense as the story progresses. Refer to this to keep you on track.)

Personal:_____

_____

_____

Public:_____

_____

_____

Ultimate: _____

_____

_____

Angle
(Look at the *Angle Worksheet*. Write out what makes your book unique. Play into that as you work.)

_____

_____

_____

_____

_____

_____

_____

Storytelling Decisions

Point of View and Narration

(Use the *Point of View Worksheet* and the *Narration Worksheet* to determine how you will tell the story. List out the POV and tense, along with any important notes about your choices.)

_____

_____

_____

_____

_____

Rules and Promises

(Use the *Setting the Rules For Your World Worksheet* and *Promises to the Reader Worksheet* to determine what is most important in your story. Write the things you don't want to forget here.)

_____

_____

_____

_____

_____

_____

_____

_____

_____

Character

Named Characters

(Copy over the major characters from your *Named Characters List*. Add the two most important things about each one that you uncovered in the other character worksheets. Use this as you work to make sure you aren't neglecting anyone. Verify they all have agency.)

_____
_____
_____
_____
_____
_____
_____
_____
_____
_____
_____
_____
_____
_____
_____
_____
_____
_____

Setting/Worldbuilding

Big Picture Location
(Provide details about the country, planet, or geographic region where your story is set.)

_____

_____

_____

_____

_____

_____

Small Picture Locations
(List each interior or exterior location in your story. Think carefully about whether you need them all or if any could be combined.)

_____

_____

_____

_____

_____

_____

_____

_____

Worldbuilding

(List out the aspects of worldbuilding you plan to include in your book. If there is additional information (charts, graphs or detailed explanations of how something works) that won't fit in your list, note what it is and where it is located.)

_____

_____

_____

_____

_____

_____

_____

_____

_____

_____

_____

_____

_____

_____

_____

_____

_____

Graphics

(Make a list of any additional maps, diagrams, schematics, coat of arms, sketches, interior layouts, etc. you have created. Decide how you will keep track of them. Note beside each one where it is located.)

_____

_____

_____

_____

_____

_____

Plot

Scenes in Progress

(Write out the key points from your plot. Note beside them what aspects you need to work on. Update this as you work.)

_____

_____

_____

_____

_____

_____

_____

_____

Timelines

Timeline
(Draw out any timelines important to your story – surrounding history, personal character milestones, etc.)

Questions:

(Keep a running list of things you need to know. Jot down things as you write. That way, you won't interrupt your writing flow, but you also won't forget to go back and verify things later.

_____

_____

_____

_____

_____

_____

_____

_____

Research

Bibliography

(Keep a running list of each resource you consult to verify information as you work. This will come in handy when you go to re-check things or find related information.) Add important notes here.

_____

_____

_____

_____

_____

Do You Need a Full Story Bible? Checklist

Concerns

❒ Are you having trouble understanding your characters, or making your plot or characters interesting?

❒ Is your book too long? Too short?

❒ Are you starting a new manuscript and aren't quite sure where to go with it?

❒ Are you having trouble boiling down what your book is really about?

❒ Do you want to double-check that you are writing everything consistently?

Aspects

❒ Is this story going to span more than one volume?

❒ Do you have a large cast of characters?

❒ Is your book a saga spanning generations?

❒ Is the backstory complicated?

❒ Are you going to have to do painstaking historical research?

❒ Does your story involve time travel, alternate history, alternate reality or parallel worlds?

❒ Are you creating non-human races or fictional countries?

❒ Are you including monsters, made-up planets or superpowers?

❒ Are you inventing technology?

❒ Do you have one or more characters with a complicated hobby, collections of something, or a medical condition?

❒ Do you have a story that takes place in a hospital, police station, spy organization, or somewhere else where there is a lot of jargon or technical language?

❒ Are you writing in a shared world or working with a collaborator?

Named Characters List

	Name	Name Meaning	Nickname(s)	Role in Story
1				
2				
3				
4				
5				
6				
7				
8				
9				
10				
11				
12				
13				
14				
15				

Invented Objects and Places List

A. Objects

Object	What is It?	Uses	Role in Story
1			
2			
3			
4			
5			
6			
7			
8			
9			
10			
11			
12			
13			
14			
15			

B. Places

Place	Where is It?	History Factoid	Role in Story
1			
2			
3			
4			
5			
6			
7			
8			
9			
10			
11			
12			
13			
14			
15			

Narration Worksheet

Narrator

Who will tell your story? _____

Is this person:

❏ The protagonist

❏ A separate character who interacts with the protagonist

❏ Multiple characters in alternating first person chapters

❏ Multiple characters in alternating third person chapters

❏ An omniscient outsider

❏ The author, in some meta capacity (or other experimental-form narrator)

How trustworthy is this narrator? _____

_____

How self-aware is this narrator? _____

_____

Frame Structure

Is there a framing narrative?

❏ None

❏ Bookends (different timeline, before and after)

❏ Prologue

❏ Epilogue

If yes, why do you need it? _____

_____

What happens to the narrator after the story ends? _____

_____

Tense

How current is the narration?

☐ As events are happening (present tense)

☐ As a reflection of what happened to the narrator a long time ago (past tense, possibly bookended with present tense)

☐ In the recent past

☐ In medias res

☐ Future, out of timeline order, or other experimental-form tense

How does this timing affect how you plan to tell the story? _____

_____

How will you make any non-chronological elements make sense? _____

_____

_____

Tone

What tone will the narration take?

☐ Somber, Dramatic   ☐ Optomistic

☐ Lighthearted   ☐ Pessimistic

☐ Humorous   ☐ Other:

☐ Lyrical, Poetic   _____

Technique

Will you employ:

☐ Deep POV (going inside the narrator's mind and heart)

☐ Stream of consciousness (flowing thoughts)

Point of View Worksheet

Scope

Is your story: ❏ Intimate   ❏ Sweeping

Do you have: ❏ A small cast of characters   ❏ A large cast of characters

Is this the story of love between two people, or an epic tale with the entire world at stake? Somewhere in between? Chart this along the dotted line on the graph below.

Interior Life

How much of your story is interior to your characters?
❏ A good deal ❏ Very little

How deeply will you explore the characters' thoughts and feelings on an internal level? Going from the most (left) to least (right) chart your story along the horizontal axis on the graph below.

External Narration

How much of your story is observable from outside your characters heads?
❏ A good deal ❏ Very little

If your story was made into a movie, how much could remain the same? Going from bottom (most) to top (least) chart your story on the graph below.

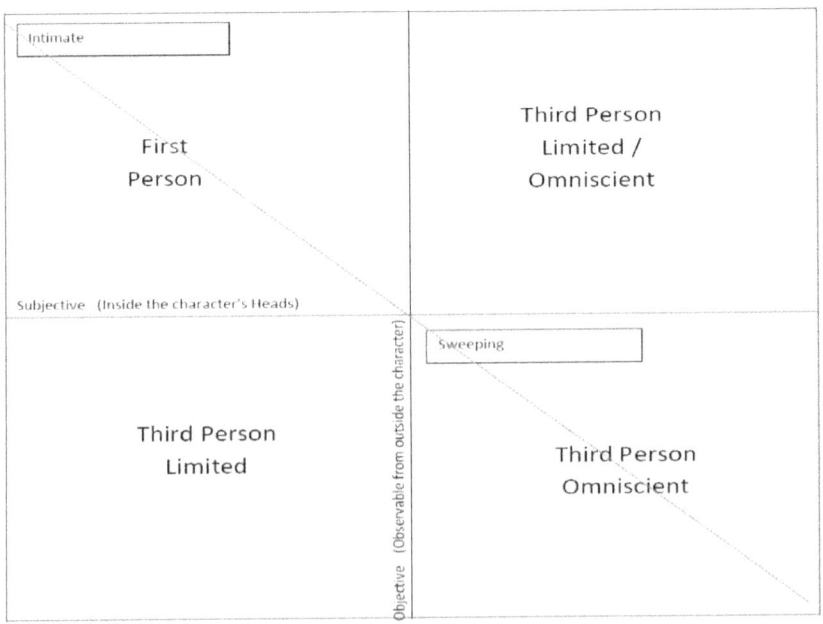

A-5

© Amber Royer 2020

Setting Rules for Your World Worksheet

Genre

What genre expectations should readers find in your book?

☐ Literary Fiction: Plumbs the character's psyche, tragic endings allowed.

☐ Commercial Fiction: Needs a "Hollywood" ending.

☐ Women's Fiction: Character growth is a must, but tragic/failed romances allowed.

☐ Historical Fiction: Takes place in another time period, and characters speak/dress/behave believably for people living in said time period.

☐ Romance: Two characters overcome challenges to achieve a Happily Ever After or Happy Enough for Now ending.

☐ Cozy Mystery: Mildly described violence leads an amateur sleuth to mild peril before bringing the culpret to light.

☐ Mystery: Grittier violence, but justice is still served in the end.

☐ Thriller: Breakneck packing and surprising plot twists (almost) always lead to the character stopping further violence and uncovering truth. Can include a twist ending.

☐ Horror: Characters fight to stop the violence, but their efforts are meaningless. A few probably survive through luck or problem solving.

☐ Speculative Fiction: The world contains a speculation about future or alternate reality. Can be science fiction or fantasy – or something harder to define. Characters are in some sense explorers in their own worlds.

☐ Young Adult Fiction: Characters are high-school age. They are experiencing "firsts" and coming of age character arcs no matter what genre the story fits.

What Genre Codes and Conventions Will this Story Follow? _____

_____

_____

_____

Safety

Which types of characters are safe from violence in your story world?

❒ Everybody

❒ Children

❒ Animals

❒ Innocents

❒ Plucky comic relief

❒ Only these characters:

    Name _____

    Name _____

    Name _____

❒ Nobody, baby. Nobody.

Intensity

What will be the level of violence in your book?

❒ None   ❒ Offscreen/Not Vividly Described   ❒ Graphic

What will be the level of romance in your book?

❒ None/Sweet   ❒ Offscreen/Not Vividly Described   ❒ Graphic

Real-World Influence

Does history/geography/science work the same in you book world as they do in the real world?

❒ Yes! I'll refer to the research worksheets.

❒ Of course not! I need to fill out the other pages of this worksheet.

Unique Rules

Point 1: _____

_____

Because of this:

A. _____

_____

B. _____

_____

C. _____

_____

D. _____

_____

Point 2: _____

_____

Because of this:

A. _____

_____

B. _____

_____

C. _____

_____

D. _____

_____

Point 3: _____

_____

Because of this:

A. _____

_____

B. _____

_____

C. _____

_____

D. _____

_____

Point 4: _____

_____

Because of this:

A. _____

_____

B. _____

_____

C. _____

_____

D. _____

_____

Determining Ease Worksheet

How is the use of technology viewed in this society? _____
_____
_____

How easy is communication? Will anything unforeseen keep your characters from communicating? _____
_____
_____

How easy is travel? (Can include through space and time) Will anything keep your characters from getting where they want to go? _____
_____
_____

If violence is committed, how easy is the method? (Could just anyone do it? How easy is it to get away with it? Or does it require expertise that would limit suspects?) _____
_____

If a specific kind of medical help is needed, how easy would it be for someone untrained to administer it? _____
_____

If the character is an expert in a trade, how long did it take to become so? How is this character/trade viewed? _____
_____

Promises to the Reader Worksheet

Your 5-Ws Promises

WHO is your protagonist? _____
_____
_____

WHAT is the problem/conflict/central thing this story is about? _____
_____
_____

WHEN does your story take place? _____
_____
_____

WHERE does your story take place? _____
_____
_____

HOW will the plot play out? (Just a quick overview) _____
_____
_____

WHY will readers remember your story? _____
_____
_____

Additional Promises

Promise 1: _____

_____

How is it relevant to your main story (your 5Ws)? _____

_____

Payoff: _____

_____

❏ Requires a subplot ❏ Introduces new characters

❏ Serves as a McGuffin/red-herring/plot twist ❏ Determines genre

❏ Determines setting ❏ Determines anticipated levels of violence

Rank the importance of this promise in relation to the others you plan to make:

_____

Promise 2: _____

_____

How is it relevant to your main story (your 5Ws)? _____

_____

Payoff: _____

_____

❏ Requires a subplot ❏ Introduces new characters

❏ Serves as a McGuffin/red-herring/plot twist ❏ Determines genre

❏ Determines setting ❏ Determines anticipated levels of violence

Rank the importance of this promise in relation to the others you plan to make:

_____

Promise 3: _____

_____

How is it relevant to your main story (your 5Ws)? _____

_____

Payoff: _____

_____

☐ Requires a subplot ☐ Introduces new characters

☐ Serves as a McGuffin/red-herring/plot twist ☐ Determines genre

☐ Determines setting ☐ Determines anticipated levels of violence

Rank the importance of this promise in relation to the others you plan to make:

_____

Promise 4: _____

_____

How is it relevant to your main story (your 5Ws)? _____

_____

Payoff: _____

_____

☐ Requires a subplot ☐ Introduces new characters

☐ Serves as a McGuffin/red-herring/plot twist ☐ Determines genre

☐ Determines setting ☐ Determines anticipated levels of violence

Rank the importance of this promise in relation to the others you plan to make:

_____

Promise 5: _____

_____

How is it relevant to your main story (your 5Ws)? _____

_____

Payoff: _____

_____

❒ Requires a subplot   ❒ Introduces new characters

❒ Serves as a McGuffin/red-herring/plot twist   ❒ Determines genre

❒ Determines setting   ❒ Determines anticipated levels of violence

Rank the importance of this promise in relation to the others you plan to make:

_____

Promise 6: _____

_____

How is it relevant to your main story (your 5Ws)? _____

_____

Payoff: _____

_____

❒ Requires a subplot   ❒ Introduces new characters

❒ Serves as a McGuffin/red-herring/plot twist   ❒ Determines genre

❒ Determines setting   ❒ Determines anticipated levels of violence

Rank the importance of this promise in relation to the others you plan to make:

_____

Who Has Agency Worksheet

Character	Meaningful Choice 1	Meaningful Choice 2	Meaningful Choice 3
1			
2			
3			
4			
5			
6			
7			

Research Questions Worksheet

Where will your manuscript touch on history? _____
_____

Where will your manuscript touch on geography? _____
_____

Where will your manuscript touch on science? _____
_____

Will this manuscript require you to know more about:

☐ Weapons: Type _____

☐ Rogue's Skills: Type _____

☐ Horses: _____

☐ Travel: _____

☐ Fashion: _____

☐ A ParticularOoccupation: _____

☐ A Particular Hobby: _____

☐ A Medical Condition: _____

☐ The Justice System: _____

☐ Another Culture: _____

☐ Psychology: _____

☐ Art/Entertainment: _____

☐ Food/Cooking: _____

☐ Foreign Language: _____

☐ Jargon: _____

☐ Weather: _____

Bibliography Worksheet

Source Citation	
Key Information	Notes

Source Citation	
Key Information	Notes

Source Citation	
Key Information	Notes

Source Citation	
Key Information	Notes

Source Citation	
Key Information	Notes

Source Citation	
Key Information	Notes

Source Citation	
Key Information	Notes

Source Citation	
Key Information	Notes

Source Citation	
Key Information	Notes

Real World Story Idea List

Idea: _____

Source: _____

Idea: _____

Source: _____

Idea: _____

Source: _____

Idea: _____

Source: _____

Idea: _____

Source: _____

Idea: _____

Source: _____

Idea: _____

Source: _____

Idea: _____

Source: _____

Idea Generation Worksheet

Realistic Stories (Contemporary or Historical)

☐ A character leaves home and has to figure out how to live on their own.

☐ A character finds out their romantic relationship isn't in the state they thought it was (positive or negative).

☐ A character suffers a tragic loss.

☐ A group of friends bonds over a shared experience.

☐ A character returns to their hometown.

☐ A character who dislikes children has to take care of one.

☐ A family experiences parallel problems over several generations.

☐ A character goes from rags to riches/riches to rags.

☐ A character has to deal with the realities of war.

☐ A character has to deal with a crisis caused by mental illness.

☐ A character helps a loved one fight an addiction.

☐ A character becomes obsessed with a particular art/music form.

☐ A character has serious problems with their neighbors/townsfolk.

☐ A character hosts a series of underground art/food/activist events.

☐ A character uncovers a family secret.

☐ A character escapes an abusive relationship.

☐ A character gets mistaken for someone else.

☐ A character is in an accident, and must deal with a sudden change in abilities.

☐ A character makes new "friends" and winds up on a self-destructive path.

☐ A character seeks out a mentor, and finds the thing they want to learn is more difficult than they thought.

☐ A character is diagnosed with a terminal illness.

☐ A character takes a DNA test and gets unexpected results.

Mystery/Thriller/Horror Stories

- ☐ A character searches for an artifact or hidden treasure.
- ☐ A character uncovers a secret message from the past.
- ☐ A character uncovers a conspiracy.
- ☐ A character is invited to join a spy/police organization.
- ☐ A group of characters plan a heist.
- ☐ A character solves a murder/series of murders.
- ☐ A group of characters investigates something that doesn't make sense.
- ☐ A group of characters looks for a missing person.
- ☐ A character gets abducted/becomes a hostage.
- ☐ A character discovers significant gaps in their memory.
- ☐ A character sees something they wish they could unsee.
- ☐ A character has a stalker.
- ☐ A character's identity is stolen.
- ☐ A character starts spying on their odd new neighbors/workmate.
- ☐ A character is framed for murder.
- ☐ A character fakes their own death.
- ☐ A character is blackmailing others.
- ☐ A character goes undercover in a criminal organization.
- ☐ A character's scientific/genealogical research is suspiciously destroyed.
- ☐ A character starts therapy for disturbing dreams.
- ☐ A character wakes up in the psych ward/covered with blood/holding a weapon.
- ☐ A character overhears someone planning a crime.
- ☐ A character becomes part of an in-group . . . and then finds out the group's true agenda.

Romance Stories

- ☐ A character who doesn't believe in love meets someone special.
- ☐ A character falls in love with someone who seems wrong for them.
- ☐ Two characters enter a marriage of convenience.
- ☐ Two characters start as enemies, but fall in love.
- ☐ Two characters both want the same object/job/honor.
- ☐ A character re-encounters an old flame.
- ☐ A character receives an accidental e-mail – and starts a conversation.
- ☐ A character realizes they are in love with their best friend.
- ☐ A character is rescued from an accident or kidnapping by a mysterious stranger/firefighter/cowboy/billionaire.
- ☐ A character must choose who to be with in a love triangle.
- ☐ Two characters fall in love in different time periods.
- ☐ A character lies at the beginning of a relationship.
- ☐ A character breaks up with their love interest – only to realize it was a mistake.
- ☐ A character falls in love with someone who may – or may not – be a killer.
- ☐ A character discovers a cache of old love letters.
- ☐ A character takes a trip to a foreign country.
- ☐ A character receives an unexpected inheritance.
- ☐ A character finds themselves in need of police protection/a bodyguard.
- ☐ Two characters are trapped in a disaster and have to work together to survive.
- ☐ A character falls in love with an alien/other speculative love interest/spy.
- ☐ Two characters make horrible first impressions on each other.
- ☐ A character who was faking a relationship actually falls in love.
- ☐ An expected romance dynamic is flipped (*Example:* SHE's the cop).

Speculative Fiction Stories

☐ An AI gains sentience.

☐ A character finds a device but cannot figure out its use.

☐ A character travels through time.

☐ A character goes through a portal into another world.

☐ A character navigates a dystopian world.

☐ A character from a fantastic world has an adventure.

☐ A character has an adventure in an alternate timeline.

☐ A character's life parallels a fairy tale.

☐ A humble character finds out they are the chosen one.

☐ A group of characters face some kind of monsters.

☐ A group of characters explore/save/wage war in the galaxy.

☐ A character makes a scientific discovery that changes how humans live.

☐ A character becomes a superhero.

☐ A character relives the same day over again.

☐ A character is rescued by an opposing clan/species/cell.

☐ A character's special ability becomes a curse.

☐ A character meets themselves (clone, doppelganger, etc.).

☐ A character receives a letter in an unknown language.

☐ A character embarks on a quest.

☐ A character is given a book from the future/alternate past/another realm.

☐ A character finds themselves at the center of court/galactic intrigue.

☐ A character finds themselves in a First Contact situation.

☐ A character must figure out why something inexplicable has happened to the planet.

☐ A character has an archnemesis.

Young Adult Stories

☐ A group of teen characters deal with an issue like abuse or suicide.

☐ A teen character deals with their parents' divorce.

☐ A teen character's love interest is murdered/abducted.

☐ A group of teen characters have to save the world.

☐ Two teen characters are forced to move apart.

☐ A teen character has to deal with the effects of a rumor.

☐ A teen character has a coming of age experience.

☐ A teen character starts at a new school.

☐ A teen character is rejected for early admission to college.

☐ A teen character loses a pet.

☐ A group of teen characters go somewhere they have been told is off limits.

☐ A teen character accepts a dare that gets out of hand.

☐ A teen character is asked to do something that leaves them morally conflicted.

☐ A teen character's foster parents want to adopt them.

☐ A teen character is stranded in the wilderness.

☐ A teen character loses everything in a disaster.

☐ A teen character gets caught cheating or committing a petty crime.

☐ A teen character finds and abandoned purse/backpack/briefcase and opens it.

☐ A teen character gets lost inside a virtual reality simulation.

☐ A teen character becomes obsessed with a certain period of history.

☐ A family deals with an unexpected occurrence.

☐ A teen characters' parents are accused of a crime.

☐ A teen character takes a first job – that isn't exactly what was advertised.

Specific Ideas

Angle Worksheet

Name eight books published in the past 5 years with some similarity to yours.

1. _____
2. _____
3. _____
4. _____
5. _____
6. _____
7. _____
8. _____

What sets your protagonist apart from the protagonists of all of these?
_____.

What sets your narrative voice apart from the narrators of all of these?
_____.

What sets your setting apart from the settings of all of these?
_____.

What sets your (romance/how-done-it/speculative element) apart from the genre elements of all of these?
_____.

How will your story say something new in your genre's conversation?
_____.

How will your story flip the expected tropes of your genre?
_____.

What makes you the only person who can tell your story quite this way?
_____.

Genre Conversations Worksheet

What has your genre said in the past about your book's topic? _____

_____

_____

_____

_____

_____

What do you want to re-interpret? _____

_____

_____

_____

_____

What do you want to build on? _____

_____

_____

_____

_____

What do you want to comment on? _____

_____

_____

_____

_____

How do you want to flip/reenvision your genre's tropes? _____

_____

_____

_____

_____

How do you want to reimagine your genre's character types/species/etc.? ____

_____

_____

_____

_____

What do you want to add to your genre's conversation about love, justice, speculation about the future, or whatever your genre explores? _____

_____

_____

_____

_____

What do you love about your genre and would never change? _____

_____

_____

_____

_____

Idea Mashups Worksheet

List 5 characters you like, and what you find interesting about them.

1. _____

   _____

2. _____

   _____

3. _____

   _____

4. _____

   _____

5. _____

   _____

List 5 stories you have enjoyed, and which parts you liked best.

1. _____

   _____

2. _____

   _____

3. _____

   _____

4. _____

   _____

5. _____

   _____

List 5 settings you have seen used well, and what you like about them.

1. _____
_____

2. _____
_____

3. _____
_____

4. _____
_____

5. _____
_____

List 5 genre elements/tropes you are a sucker for and why.

1. _____
_____

2. _____
_____

3. _____
_____

4. _____
_____

5. _____
_____

Create 5 story ideas that combine elements from the above, or take one element you like and add a twist (in the vein of *Movie at Location* or *Movie with Character Type*).

1. _____
_____

2. _____
_____

3. _____
_____

4. _____
_____

5. _____
_____

Take your original novel idea and write out what the idea would become if you added in each of your new ideas to create a mashup premise.

1. _____
_____

2. _____
_____

3. _____
_____

4. _____
_____

5. _____
_____

Novelist's Lede Worksheet

Rewrite the opening sentences of your story to highlight the dramatic action. Make sure there is something at stake for the characters.

_____

_____

_____

_____

_____

_____

Rewrite the opening sentences of your story to highlight a mysterious aspect of your setting. A character should actively be engaging with this aspect of the setting.

_____

_____

_____

_____

_____

_____

Rewrite the opening sentences of your story to highlight a choice your protagonist has to make. Make sure this takes place in the middle of an active scene.

_____

_____

_____

_____

_____

_____

Rewrite the opening sentences of your story to foreshadow the thematic statement you plan to make at the climax of your story.

_____

_____

_____

_____

_____

_____

Rewrite the opening sentences of your story to raise a question in the reader's mind (usually a WHAT or WHY question – *Example:* What will this character do to escape being stuck in an elevator, or Why did that character just get kidnapped). Make sure the question is raised as part of an active scene.

_____

_____

_____

_____

_____

_____

Rewrite the opening sentences of your story. Start with a startling statement designed to shock or surprise the reader. The following sentences should give context to this statement, in the middle of an active scene.

_____

_____

_____

_____

_____

_____

Rewrite the opening sentences of your story to include a statement of your topic – be it found family, time travel, or who killed Mr. McGreggor – in the style Jane Austen used to open Pride and Prejudice (It is a truth generally acknowledged . . .). This should only take one sentence, and should be part of an active scene.

_____
_____
_____
_____
_____
_____
_____

Rewrite the opening sentences of your story so that the narrator is making an observation about human nature or society based on the events taking place in the opening scene.

_____
_____
_____
_____
_____
_____
_____
_____
_____
_____
_____
_____

Imagery Worksheet

I can see . . .	I can hear . . .	I can touch . . .
I can smell . . .	I can taste . . .	Descriptive words that come to mind are . . .
My body moves . . .	I feel (hunger, pain, etc.) . . .	My reaction is . . .

Use the sensory inputs to write a paragraph.

Body Language Observation Worksheet

Observation 1

_____ + _____ + _____ = _____
(body language)   (body language)   (body language)   (emotion)

Observation 2

_____ + _____ + _____ = _____
(body language)   (body language)   (body language)   (emotion)

Observation 3

_____ + _____ + _____ = _____
(body language)   (body language)   (body language)   (emotion)

Observation 4

_____ + _____ + _____ = _____
(body language)   (body language)   (body language)   (emotion)

Observation 5

_____ + _____ + _____ = _____
(body language)   (body language)   (body language)   (emotion)

Observation 6

_____ + _____ + _____ = _____
(body language)   (body language)   (body language)   (emotion)

Observation 7

_____ + _____ + _____ = _____
(body language)   (body language)   (body language)   (emotion)

Observation 8

_____ + _____ + _____ = _____
(body language)   (body language)   (body language)   (emotion)

Observation 9

_____ + _____ + _____ = _____
(body language)   (body language)   (body language)   (emotion)

Observation 10

_____ + _____ + _____ = _____
(body language)   (body language)   (body language)   (emotion)

Story Body Language 1

_____
_____
_____
_____
_____
_____
_____
_____

Story Body Language 2

_____
_____
_____
_____
_____
_____
_____
_____
_____
_____

Story Body Language 3

_____
_____
_____
_____
_____
_____
_____
_____
_____

Blocking Worksheet

Up Stage — Stage Left — Down Stage — Stage Right

Storyboarding Worksheet

A-21

© Amber Royer 2020

Language Overview Worksheet

What languages are spoken in this setting?

_____   _____

_____   _____

_____   _____

Are any of them dialects? ❐ Yes ❐ No

Are any of them invented languages?

❐ Yes! I'll fill out the lexicon worksheet.

❐ No. I'm good with existing dictionaries.

How many languages does the average person speak? _____

How much education does the average person receive? _____

_____

_____

Can everyone read? ❐ Yes ❐ No

Can everyone write? ❐ Yes ❐ No

Is any class/type of people prohibited from learning any of the languages spoken here? ❐ Yes ❐ No

If yes, which language and why? _____

_____

Is there a common language used for diplomacy/trade? ❐ Yes ❐ No

How well does it work? (Are there still frequent misunderstandings?) How many people know it? _____

_____

Lexicon Worksheet

Syntax

How does the sense of self/community and ideas about objects and ownerships affect this language group's sentence structure? Rate the importance of:

Subject _____   Object _____

Verbs (actions)_____   Descriptors (adjectives)_____

Modifiers (adverbs)_____   Other _____

Is the sentence structure similar to a known language? ❑ Yes ❑ No

If yes, then which one? _____

If not, is a basic sentence structure:

❑ Subject verb object. (She petted the cat.)

❑ Subject object verb. (She the cat petted.)

❑ Verb subject object. (Petted she the cat.)

❑ Object subject verb. (The cat she petted.)

❑ Other _____

What linguistic rules govern language construction? (including verb conjugation, presence/absence of articles or subject markers, word suffixes and prefixes, and language tense) _____

_____

_____

_____

_____

Mindset

What natural phenomena and intellectual concepts are most important to these people?

_____   _____

_____   _____

What words would be most important to them based on the above answers? How might they have multiple words for topics related to these things?

_____   _____

_____   _____

_____   _____

_____   _____

_____   _____

_____   _____

How do they view things like property and time? What words do they use for these?

_____   _____

_____   _____

_____   _____

How do they use numbers? Binary, Decimal, Hexadecimal?

_____   _____

What are their impolite words?

_____   _____

_____   _____

General Vocabulary and Word Meaning

Jargon Worksheet

What jargon does your character use and what does it mean?

_____   _____
_____   _____
_____   _____
_____   _____
_____   _____
_____   _____
_____   _____
_____   _____
_____   _____
_____   _____

Is this because of a social group, an occupation, or something else?

_____
_____

Is this understood by most everyone or does this create a sort of dialect?

_____
_____

How much of your character's speech is jargon?

_____
_____

Word Choice Chart

Generic Words	Character 1 Where am I from? What do I do? Most of the time, I feel:	Character 2 Where am I from? What do I do? Most of the time, I feel:	Character 3 Where am I from? What do I do? Most of the time, I feel:

www.ingramcontent.com/pod-product-compliance
Lightning Source LLC
Chambersburg PA
CBHW060425010526
44118CB00017B/2368